Gallery Books
Editor: Peter Fallon

THE HARPER'S TURN

Tom Mac Intyre

The Harper's Turn

with an introduction by **Seamus Heaney**

 Gallery Books

The Harper's Turn
is published first
in July 1982
in paperback and in
a clothbound edition.

The Gallery Press
19 Oakdown Road
Dublin 14
Ireland.

Cover design by Michael Kane

ISBN 0 904011 29 1 (*clothbound*)
     0 904011 30 5 (*paperback*)

Acknowledgements are due to the editors of *The Drumlin, The Dubliner, Etudes Irlandaises, New Irish Writing* (The Irish Press), *The New World Journal* and *Winter's Tales from Ireland,* to Faber and Faber Ltd., and to BBC Radio Three and RTE.
The Gallery Press acknowledges gratefully the assistance of An Chomhairle Ealaíon (The Arts Council of Ireland) towards the publication of this book.

Contents

Introduction

I have not grasped the full import and the inner logic of all the stories in this book and cannot, indeed, be sure that 'stories' is the word to use about all of them. But that does not matter. With the publication of this selection of Tom Mac Intyre's shorter works, we are saluting a writer *nel mezzo del cammin*.

Yet he is not, after all, a middle of the road writer. He corners at speed, instinctively accelerating away from what Joseph Brodsky has called the 'aesthetic inertia' that is always threatening the professional writer of prose. There is a far thing, pierced and lonely, some crystal of hurt transmitting a pure signal. A few pieces reminded me of the hedged and elusive intensities of the Eliot of *The Waste Land,* that sense of antic conjuring, a plot withheld but a probe going out. And what Eliot later sought as he struggled with *Little Gidding* seems to have been found in many places by Tom Mac Intyre, 'some acute personal reminiscence (never to be explicated, of course, but to give power from well below the surface)'.

Whoever it was defined writing as nervous energy translated into phrases might have been thinking of this writer's first talent. It was in the cell of the phrase that Mac Intyre's energy beat from the start. I remember my elation when *'Stallions'* first appeared almost twenty years ago in *The Dubliner* (it was then called *'At Twelve the Marketyard'*) and though we can now see that story and the one that follows it in this collection as relatively conventional in the context of this writer's later work, we can also see, twenty years and a wilderness of short stories later, why his name figures in the very short list of Irish writers who have set out to make it new.

There is another exemplary feature of the career: a pursuit of impulse, an indifference to conventional literary success, a risk-taking. With *The Charollais* (1969) and *Dance The Dance* (1970) 'hailed', as they say, he could have 'followed up'.

Instead, he pitched *Through the Bridewell Gate* into the Dublin Arms Trial, then swerved into the theatre, sailing close to the rocks of 'engagement' while following the star of some inner commitment. 'You know', said Frost, 'the real thing is that the sense of sacrifice and risk is one of the greatest stimuli in the world.' So next he went further and nearly abjured language altogether for the gesture of the dance, and it is from that stage- and troupe-work that here springs some of the more elliptical (and still, to my mind, less persuasive) pieces in this book. But perhaps it was the exposure to the footlights which extended him beyond the burning-glass focus of the phrase; the new animating element at work here is the shape-shifting, submarine half-light of myth.

When Irish mythology began to become a literary currency at the end of the nineteenth century, it was used to vindicate a claim to national identity, historic culture, spiritual resource. A hundred years later the writer approaches it with less propagandist intent, with a primary hunger for form, in order to find structure for unstructured potential within himself. Thus, *'The Man-Keeper'*, while it could be said to demonstrate 'the riches of the folk tradition', should also be seen as a pure exultation in fluency and inventiveness *per se*; it is, in its modern way, distanced from itself by knowing what makes itself tick. Yet it is still free in an objective enjoyment of its own energies and is not niggardly with speech or incident in the way that some other pieces seem to be.

In fact, the drama we are witnessing in this book is a conflict between two strains of narrative, two contradictory imperatives. One says, 'Tell it all, let it run, enjoy the spill of words'; the other says, 'Withhold, cut back, condense'. In pieces like *'The Hurt Mind'* and *'Occasion of Note'*, this tension between tale-telling and shape-making is just about held, but in many of the others it is the shape-making faculty that wins out strongest and the mythic lineaments insist on their presence as reminder —or projection—of the archetype. And this is why I wonder if 'story' is, after all, the term for everything here. Language left to play so autonomously is reaching for the condition of poetry.

Seamus Heaney

9

for **Kathryn**

Stallions

One afternoon the housekeeper pounced—
—You're going to the creamery, the can pushed at me, two shillings worth of cream and hurry back.

I went down the avenue and on to the road where tar oozed and gleamed after hours of sun.

The town lay a good shout off, the creamery half a mile beyond. I set out, past Jack Traynor's who had been a schoolmaster, was now old, and came abroad only to walk in the downpour; past Miss Farnan's who snatched kindling from behind hedges and had seen The Blessed Virgin; past Tom Millar's who housed a motor-bike and greyhounds but was Protestant. I stopped at Carroll's archway, that day a funnel of shadows. My eyes pricked. Among the shadows, sloping 'round the curve which hid the gap of the other end, was Albert McElwaine.

There was something up in Carroll's yard.

McElwaine was about my age, his curiosity mine. The cut of him lured me, the lie of his back, the drag of his hand as he took the bend—blurring himself to the wall. I followed, hastening through, round the blind curve and into the yard, a square, which held the light like a bowl.

Ten or twenty men were standing about, talking in groups, smoking, testing the ground with ashplants or nubbly blackthorns. A line of carts to one side, cherry and blue, shafts down, backsides up, harness slack in their bellies, had gone to sleep. There was a green whiff of droppings, and the stomping and tossing of horses fidgety in the dark stables. Nothing was happening. McElwaine, by himself in a far corner, hadn't seen me yet.

From behind the row of carts, someone brought out a black mare, shivery patches of sweat slick on her rump. In the middle of the yard they stopped, waiting, the middle their own. The space had grown while they moved into it. The mare jibbed and

11

wheeled.

As if a thousand locks had snapped, a door to the left flew open. A stallion ricochetted into the sun, pawed for the sky, and let out a whinny that flared over the town.

Excited and glancing, the mare waited. For the first time, I saw the ostler, puny, and the reins. Flanks in a quiver, the stallion broke forward, closed, reared and plunged. Guiding in the reek and sweat flashed the red hand of the ostler. The stallion, straddled, pumped like his taut hamstrings must split. Then the ostler again, parting them, the spill passed on. The mare was led away. Snorting and champing, the chestnut was stalled.

Again the butt of a hobnailed boot, a farmer near me rapped his pipe.

—Well, boy, what d'ye make of it?

He grinned down over a porter belly.

Flushed and floundering, I left.

Every Monday I escaped to the yard. McElwaine was always there. And a few others I knew in school. Here we never spoke. Singly, privately, we awaited each loud unbolting and the rush that followed. It was like watching the start of the world.

Curried and ribboned and bobbed, the stallion roiled my dreams.

I saw the future: fifty-two Mondays bright and luscious in the year.

On my fourth visit, Lil Carroll, ladling sugar into two-pound bags, looked out a spidery window, saw me criminal among the men. And told.

When Mother called I was eating in the kitchen.

—Come up here you.

Fearful, I rose and followed her up to the parlour.

First she stood with her back to me, staring out on the flower-garden, said nothing. Then she turned, making a slow sign of the cross, and met me with a dead face.

—Where were you this afternoon?

—Playing football.

—Football! she mocked, in Carroll's yard?

I eyed the garden behind her.

—May, she said, Our Lady's Month.

I shrank to a culprit.

—If I ever hear of you being there again, you'll get a dose you won't forget.

—Promise, she commanded, come on.

—I promise.

There was a pause while she studied me, and with it I could feel driving between us the fury of the yard, the glare and the ripeness, the sling of the door's opening, the stallion loosed again.

—Go back to your tea.

I left the room.

—Stallions, I heard her say on my way down the hall.

Boarding

On Thursday at three I stood before Clongowes. The barbered
frontage, two-thirds ivied, shone even in the downpour. I
sprinted the gravel, swung back the smooth-rolling oak door,
and stepped inside. In the sparse light of the shallow hall-way
stone and iron, four teak doors, and a baroque Ignatius
reaching for his sword.
—You're the man come to meet Father Naughton?
The butler, skipping yield of a recess to the right.
—Yes.
—This way. Desperate summer. Cows swimming on dry
land these parts.
No-age joker, small, ox-necked.
—And hay-cocks sailing for the sea.
A lift in his voice hoisted him abroad one, carried us both
to the first landing, his dark jaw, dark livery, tangy with the
salt of misrule.
—This way now.
We were rising into the body of the castle, up cranky stairs
and along the porous silence of low windowless corridors. I
recall: the broad back climbing, saints and martyrs in wood
and plaster and great coughing canvases of the romantic decline,
bags of shadow, the continuing ascent, still the broad back
there a yard or two ahead but remote, the surround distancing
us as it pleased.
—Here you are, Sir.
A room opening to me.
—He'll be with you shortly, Sir.
Sirs now.
—And if there's anything you need, Sir.
—Thank you, Sir.
In the room prayer and penance hung about like chewed
bones. And what next under God, Ignatius, The Black Pope,
and imminent Father Naughton? Minutes passed, and my hand

14

drew open the drawer of a desk. A blotched page from an old hand-book. Without moving it, I read—

1180 Clongowes and Rathcoffey in the Mainham Estate of Adam de Hereford.
1415 Probable date of the first large castle.
1493 Clongowes formally granted to the Eustaces, Viscounts Baltinglass.
1542 Jesuits first came to Ireland.
1641 Eustaces of Clongowes join Confederate revolt.
1642 Clongowes Castle captured and demolished by troops of General Monk.
1718 Castle restored by Stephen Fitzwilliam Browne.
1813 Castle and Estate bought by the Jesuits.

Shutting the drawer I stood there. And a bald little priest spun into the room as if a squadron jigged at his heels.

—Hello. How are you? You're very welcome—he engaged my hand, disposed of it—Sit down, won't you? Well now, the position is this—

Father Harold Naughton, S.J., tea-rose face fresh above the tended soutane and the laughing shoes, marched the room and dealt me the stunning irrelevancies of the mighty.

—We have three-hundred boys in the place, he said on the swivel, teeth trifling with a smile. The cream of the country—rich and thick.

—We may ask you to teach anything, he said, rolling the balls of his feet. From Hebrew to Hindustani. It's the system. The Minister for Education is mad.

—This place *is* isolated, he said, looking out the window through his lips, but one suicide in a hundred and fifty years is fair enough, isn't it? In any case, he went on, I don't believe that was a suicide. The fool fell into the moat.

Ten minutes of a wet and blowy afternoon in that high room of the castle on the limestone plain. Pantried somewhere below, my supple guide; de Hereford and Eustace and Fitzwilliam Browne wild in the walls, Naughton speaking on, a trim

15

survivor, a spirit—fire and steel—that sang as the bullet sings.
And I knew the rummaging curiosity of youth about to seduce
me.

—Great. Great—a short hand, polished at the joints, was
mine—Great. The population arrive on September 5th.

As I left it had stopped raining but the light had not improved.
The avenue's guard of limes, scent hesitantly lacing the murk,
attended. Stillness. No activity but for a tall priest—in his left
hand, stiffly, a slash-hook—crossing a field away to the right.
Making for the woodland.

Next evening I was back in Donegal, my lodgings the house
of a butcher on a knot of rock above the sea. The butcher's
wife was towelling my hair, talking once more of the life she'd
known as a nurse in Glasgow, putting before me the images of
her hunger and the excitements of her love.

16

Stirabout

—Ever see a king better than me?
—Never.
—Ever see a strong-man better than my strong-man?
—Never.
—Ever see men of battle better than my men of battle?
—Never.
The poet at the other end of the table—Esirt, poet to The King of The Pigmies—started laughing.
—Arrest him.
He was grabbed.
—This means trouble, said the poet.
—Trouble for you.
The poet had been to The Land of the Grown-Ups: he was paid to know more than the one world. He requested a three-day respite so that he could go there and bring back evidence . . . of other modes . . .
—By all means, said The King of the Pigmies.

—So you won't eat?
—No.
—And you won't drink?
—No.
—Well, see how you like this drink, said The King of the Grown-Ups.
He popped Esirt into the nearest goblet, his own. Everyone crowded in to see, and laughter whacked the ceiling. Flailing about in the wine, Esirt called on the poets to save him. The chief poet intervened, and he was lifted out. And mopped up.
—Now will you eat?
—When I've spoken to you, he told The King.
They stood apart.
—Your cock owns you.
The King looked at this extraordinary visitor, the size of a

17

doubled fist or slightly less, comely, and, it was plain, per-
ceptive.

—Mind yourself, said Esirt.

Over a few days, Esirt entertained, and was entertained: more
the former, they'd never come across anyone quite like him,
he made their own chief poet, Aodh, also a dwarf, seem tame.
Esirt was the smaller (he could stand on Aodh's palm, Aodh
could stand on the palm of a grown-up) but—viewing the
pair—the immediately apparent difference was that Aodh did
not have Esirt's eye. Did, by the way, the two get on? They
did, as is the manner of poets, and they didn't.

—A poem about my king, said Esirt, if I may . . .

All attended.

The poem was long and sometimes with long poems an
extract suffices.

When my king sets himself in motion, he brings death to the
brave . . .

Praise to a formula? Perhaps, but as delivered by Esirt from
his perch near a blazing fire, it had a skin of ice.

And, directly to his host:

If women have the hots for you, language cannot express, never
will express, the pitch of desire excited when my king sets himself
in motion.

Here was a brazen child—who knew far too much. There
was a rush to heap gifts. Mounds of them kept appearing, it was
the third day, the day of departure.

—Take them back. And thanks.

—We never take back gifts.

—Two-thirds for the poets then, the rest for the horse-boys.

Time to go. Aodh said he'd like to travel with him.

—Fine.

The two walked as far as the shore.

—What now? said Aodh.

—We'll be collected.

—Who'll collect us?

—My king's horse.

—I see a hare on the sea, said Aodh.

18

—That's no hare, said Esirt.

The king's horse was gold-coloured, with four green legs, crimson mane, and a long tail that floated in a permanent wave.

—He'll never manage the two of us, Aodh objected.

—Your wisdom's ponderous, Esirt came back, but you don't have to worry.

The two mounted and were carried across the sea.

—Esirt's back, and a giant with him, a messenger raced to The King of The Pigmies.

The King hurried out and gave Esirt a pinched kiss.

—You've brought a giant to destroy us, have you?

—When he's at home, said Esirt, he's a dwarf, also a poet, but be careful of him anyway. And I want a word with you.

He laid bonds on The King of The Pigmies that he must go to the land where he himself had just been, that this very night he must taste of the porridge in the porridge-pot of The King there, and, finally, he prophesied that the voyager would be away for a year and a day, and wouldn't come free without yielding the dearest thing he owned.

The King of The Pigmies turned powder at the joints. He reflected that he had started these events, and was now being pulled along in the —

—Slipstream? Esirt offered.

The King of The Pigmies studied him.

—I'll be off now, he told Esirt.

—*Bon appetit.*

He hesitated in the sooty shadow of the porridge-pot. Stood on the back of his horse, sprang, and just made it to the rim. Hauling himself up, he straddled the rim, and inspected. The porridge looked up, extensive pasture, and—not quite within reach—the shank of a silver ladle gleamed. He moved along the rim towards the ladle, positioned himself to best advantage, reached, full stretch, to grasp it—and flipped, down into the porridge, up to his navel, stuck.

Noiselessly, the horse left the premises.

19

—This one's black, the other one was fair. Who are you?
—I'm stuck.

He's stuck,
the poor divil's stuck
and he can't get out,
why didn't you shout
and you there all night?

Someone took him gently between finger and thumb, pulled.
He came clear to a languid sigh from the porridge. And they
bore him in triumph to The King.
—Another one, said The King, Who are you?
—I'm The King of The Pigmies, and I've never told a lie.
The King didn't know whether to banish him or lock him up
or what.
—Lock him up.
—Give me freedom here, The King of The Pigmies appealed,
and I promise not to leave without your consent.
The King had misgivings but he yielded.
—All right.

The visitor settled in. Everyone took to him, especially the
women—he was given the run of their bosoms, and more
intimate regions. The beaded nest, sure enough, was one of his
prime delights. He was constantly vanishing from the public
gaze, so to speak, and often it wasn't easy to decide where he
was playing because, while it's impossible to feign ecstacy,
anticipation and afterglow resemble it closely enough to
promote confusion. The King wasn't jealous nor were the men,
by and large—how could you be jealous of such a scantling,
and, besides, his presence lent an agreeable tension to the
quotidian—and the nocturnal.
—Give him time, an elder had said when he was being
labelled 'a lesser Esirt'.
He was more Esirt every day, the eye in this head also was
. . . what it was . . .

—Tell us all about the place you come from.

20

—Against man or woman that seeks to enter it that retreat is never closed.

Volumes of description, epithets from hell to Connacht, but if you want the sentence that pealed —

Against man or woman that seeks to enter it that retreat is never closed.

One evening, speaking from the mantelpiece of the main room, a great fire on the hearth below, he delivered himself with tremendous authority on the theme of what you might burn and what you might not.

Never burn the woodbine, burn not that king.
Burn not the willow, cage the bees love.
Spare the hazel, burn the briar.
Holly burn it green, holly burn it dry.

Burn green oak, the fiercest heat.
Burn the birch, stalk, pods, all.
Burn the palsied aspen.
Alder, battle-witch of all the wood, burn.

Spare the blackthorn, birds snug in that scanty body.
Bow to the whitethorn.
Burn not the apple-tree, towards whose fair head all put forth the hand.
Holly burn it green, holly burn it dry.

The army of The King of The Pigmies arrived to ask for him back. Seven battalions strong, they appeared one morning on the doorstep. They offered ransom.

—What ransom?

—To the click of a finger, we'll cover the whole plain with corn.

—I won't give him up, said The King.

—Then we'll make trouble.

—What trouble?

—We'll defile all wells, rapids, and river-mouths.

—I won't give him up.

21

They did as they'd promised and arrived again next morning
with the same demand.

—I won't give him up.

—Then we'll make trouble.

—What trouble?

—We'll burn all mill-beams and all kilns.

—I won't give him up.

They did as they'd promised and arrived again next morning
and howled for their king.

—I won't give him up.

—Then we'll make trouble.

—What trouble?

—Your women's hair, and your men's, we'll shave in such a
way that they'll be shamed forever.

The King went wild. When his advisers had calmed him, he
said that, if they did that, he, personally, would kill the one
they'd come for.

The seven battalions hushed.

And the grown-ups stood silent.

The King of The Pigmies, secured within, asked permission
to speak to his army. When he was brought to the doorstep, a
roar of victory went up: prematurely.

—Repair what you've spoiled. And go home. I'll come at
the appointed time.

So, in dismay, the army left.

The poet Aodh returned from The Land of The Pigmies.

—I have seen wonderful things.

His bearing was that of one who'd been struck dead and
kissed back to life.

—Take the spear—unconquerable in battle.

—Take the helmet—divine the future.

—Take the shoes of white bronze—they travel land and sea.

—The horse-rod—the world's women will go mad for you.

Or the shield, the cloak, the shirt, the shears, so on. The
array of minute objects shone from a handkerchief of blue silk,
each item buoyant with its own consuming magic. The King
of The Grown-Ups extended his hand, and allowed it to hover

above the treasures. He let the hand move about blindly. He dropped the hand, and came up with—the shoes.

—The treasures still endure, cried The King of The Pigmies, not so the people.

He swept up the silk handkerchief, his belongings in the middle of it. Someone caught a glimpse of the gold-coloured horse with the four green legs, the crimson mane, tail that floated in the permanent wave. Neither of them was seen again in those parts.

A tremendous row between The King and The Queen. The circumstances were banal, a question of precedence in use of the bath-stone. The King struck her, and a tooth flew.

—Fit you better, flashed The Queen, to take on The Thing of The Lake that left your mouth at the back of your head.

The King made to strike her again, at the same time shaking his head at the ground.

She left, and returned with a mirror. He looked, and saw the truth of her words.

—Why was I never told?

—We got used to it, said The Queen.

One afternoon The King and a young man of the household were walking by the lake. They stopped to bathe. While they were bathing, The Thing of The Lake appeared, and came at them. They escaped but The King was left squint-eyed and with his mouth twisted to the back of his head. No one dared mention the calamity to him. And they'd conspired to keep mirrors out of his way.

—I want a normal mouth.

—What's a normal mouth?

—A normal mouth is situate between the nose and the chin.

—Suppose the nose is off centre? Or the person chinless?

—Suppose the nose is where it should be, and the chin's a chin?

—Everybody wants one of your so-called *normal* mouths.

—Listen: my eyes squint, and my mouth's at the back of my head.

23

—Count your blessings.

—My blessings?

—You've a slight cast in one eye and your mouth tends to slip when you're tired. And you need a drink.

The King woke up very early one morning to find the shoes of white bronze on his feet. The Queen lay sleeping beside him. He slipped out of bed and into an ante-room. He tried to step out of the shoes. They wouldn't come off. He dressed quietly, took his sword, left the house, and walked down the road. He took the first bend. There was the lake.

—*Take the shoes of white bronze—they travel land and sea.*

Drawing his sword, he made for the middle of the lake. It was already seething.

They found him on the shore where he'd dragged himself to die of his wounds—but not before avenging his deformity. The lake acknowledged it. Turning from the body, they bent their eyes on the lake, and, unmistakably, they knew.

The Hurt Mind

—The Boys Who Beat The Black And Tans The Boys from
The County Cork—not quite true, not quite true, what about
Lord what about Lord Doneraile and his bucks and his blades,
I read books, what about the rights of The Big House, what
about the seed and the breed of the carriage-and-four staring
from the ditches at the carriage-and-four as the carriage-and-
four swept by, I'm talking of the hurt mind, I'm talking of the
hurt mind in wait and knowing as the hurt mind knows, the
litter of The Big House and the scatter of Captain Buck and
Major Blade, oh yes, and when The Tans came who's fightin'
who?, answer me that, the ditches fightin' their own, they're
fightin' from the hurt mind, and by the bye what about the
beagle hunt, *Come on Lord Doneraile*—I read this in a book, I
read two books a year and I read them well and one of them
had this: Fine day for a hunt, right, take a fresh young slip of
a one never touched, strip and rub all over with aniseed oil—
three scents for the beagle, hare, red herrin', aniseed oil—strip
to the pelt and rub all over and let loose, a fair start, if it's a
hunt a hunt let it be, she'll travel, she's young and supple and
she's layin' a trail and the day's long, now your beagles, now
The Lord, now Captain Buck and Major Blade, the beagles
sniffin', there's sight for you—three scents for the beagle, hare,
red herrin', aniseed oil—they've picked her scent, they've a
trail, we're away, north with her, south with her, east with her,
west with her, wasting her time and she knows it, three hours
on average the book tells me, and now they're glimpsing, flash
of her rump going through a gap, skyline cut of her, freckened
track of her, and soon they're smellin' her smellin' *her* under
the aniseed, her trail's a mile wide this minute, and now look
at them, The Lord and Captain Buck and Major Blade, now
they're lifting the croobs, now they're flying, now whose
tongue's hanging out?, listen to the beagles, where's the fresh
young slip?, lying low by the river is the fresh young slip, listen

25

to your beagles *Two to one The Captain Evens The Major* they're neck and neck in the straight, where's the fresh young slip?, she's in there hooped in the stink and the sweat and she's all thump-a-thump *Come on The Captain Tight lines Major* . . . The Captain's down! he's down, The Major's away, wins pullin' up, not pullin' up either, he's ploughin' through the scrub, wait, wait, Major gone to ground, ne'er a sound ne'er a sound *Ate up Major stop lickin' your chops* and all join in now please and thank-you, we're a musical nation, a-a-a-a-nd *The Boys Who Beat The Black And Tans Was The Boys From The County Cork!*

The Windy Tree

—How did that fairy-tale finish—do you remember?
—The king's son came up—with the ring—and made shore,
sopping wet, of course. He put the ring on a rock, and set about
drying himself. And a snake swallowed the ring. And decamped.
And that's how it finished.

—I love courage in a gambler, sir, and I see courage in your
eye, you're a gambling man and you're far from home, am I
right or am I wrong, Mrs Mulligan, you're right ma'am says
she. Find The Lady, sir, pastime old as the rocks and fresh as
dung, some say you'd want to be as quick as catching fleas by
candlelight but, sir, in reality it's simple as the sun going down.
You'll try your luck, sir, now sir, one two three and the deck
guaranteed as the jib remarked to the main-sail, and where,
sir, would you say, lies The Lady? . . . *He has a knack!* Right,
sir, you'll try a second time, you'll have a bash, your mother
won't know and I won't tell her, and one, and two, and three,
and now, sir, where, sir, would you say, lies The Lady? . . .
He has a gift! Lucky number three sang the waves of the sea,
never leave it said, sir, your father pupped a bad one, and one,
and two, and three, and now, sir, where, sir, would you say,
lies The Lady? . . . *His hand is gold!* You'll go far, sir, if you're
not hobbled, and if you don't meet rain on the road. And I'll
be with you—because I know you—from the cards, sir, it's all
in the cards, all far-and-yonder newses of the follies and the
failings of a man. . . . Oh, the maid she went to the well to
wash, Lillumwham Lillumwhey, the maid she went to the well
to wash, dew fell off her lily-white arse, Legaderry, Megaderry,
Mett, Mirr, Whoopee, Whey . . .

—This hand. It signs the documents, I thought, it rules . . .
And how clean, how spotlessly clean . . . You lifted it then to
silence the crowd—and for the first time, it seemed, I was

looking at where we live, your indifferent hand above their indifferent faces . . . I went away to my room.

—You're the born hammer, aren't you? But—whom are you hammering? Finally? And into what? You have the floor.

—Listen to me. I've been shown the other flame, the one that gives back whatever you bring to it, ice if it's ice you bring, the furnace if it's the furnace you bring.

He's finished with me. I with him. Only not quite. The crazy I detest. With good reason. *You're rocking an empty cradle,* he informs me. His pupils never dilate, I notice. Woman's hands. She won't speak to me, up to something, always are at that age. That fairy-tale, yes, I remember hearing it when I was a child. I'm turning into stretch-marks.

Morning. A servant comes as usual bearing food. I embrace the servant courteously. He jerks back, *Your beard's so rough . . . Some like it,* I joke. She happens to be passing as I say that. She blushes.

Again: I'm alone. She wanders in. She has a bucket of ice. And a bandage-roll. She sits down on the centre of the floor and, complaining of . . . shin-splints, was it?, starts to bandage her ankles with ice, at intervals looking up to question me.

My hair freshly washed, gleaming as never in life, is down over my eyes but to my surprise I can see quite clearly and the feeling is one of enormous freedom. I should let my hair down? And the eyes not seen but seeing. A primitive invisibility.

—I had a poet in the other day. Rather like you, they're all the time, obliquely or directly, going on about destiny. I put the question, perhaps I was thinking of you, *Has every man a destiny?* He answered, *Alas, no, not every man. To have a destiny you must plunge to the bottom and come up with the ring . . . Like in the fairy-tale?* I asked. *Exactly.*

—I heard that story when I was a child—a beautiful story.

—We all heard it. And my question for you, laddie, is, Have you plunged to the bottom, and have you come up with the ring? Because if not, you haven't the track of a destiny.

—If I hadn't plunged would I be here?

—But to the bottom?
—Not yet—but soon.
—Can you be so sure?
—I'm the one plunging.
—Of course . . . And will you get stuck down there? Or will you come up—with the ring—do you fancy?
—Bride to the bride-groom, I'm told.

Currently she's never to be seen without this bucket, a perfectly banal bucket, empty or containing whatever don't ask me, but without even trying she with her bucket is an *event,* everything she touches she animates, in a year or two, a month or two?, less?, her progress will be chain detonation, I heard her the other day summoning—or banishing—one of her peers, is that the word, airily *Don't call me—you've been called* clever I thought, caught the centre of her, wouldn't you agree *Don't call me—you've been called* . . .

—High hill or small room? I say that from high hills you can touch the sky. I say that in small rooms two's company. And I say red wood needs red meat.

I hung I hung on the windy tree
on the tree that none may know
on the tree that none may ever know
what root beneath it runs . . .

In the atrium the young one danced, breathing from the diaphragm, clear eyes measuring the top of the tide.

Deer Crossing

—Sire?

—Fantasy.

—'The rat who came to dinner'?

—Is this gloom?

—Fantasy, Sire, knows no gloom.

—Who told you that?

—She who taught me to suck eggs.

Clever as a clock, the jester warmed up with a hop-skip-and-jump. And took off.

—At precisely six, three evenings running, the rat came, dined, and left. The couple—happiness at risk—now took action. They fed the cat up to the whiskers—and the cat, comprehending, waited. Next evening, the rat came, there was a struggle, the cat retreated to a corner. The rat ate well, and left. Later, the cat left, and returned next day accompanied by the biggest cat you've ever seen, Sire.

Mark's right eye expanded coldly. The jester gave off sweet flavours of risk.

—The two cats were fed—up to the knob of the skull. And they waited. The rat arrived at six. They fought, Sire, for three days in the kitchen, three days in the yard, and three days on the shore. Nothing was left of the rat. The cats tidied up, strolled off arm-in-arm, and were never, Sire, seen again.

Mark's eyes were on the forest. The jester strolled, declaiming with airy intent.

—Some people ask, *What happened the couple?* And others, *What does it mean?*

Mark gone away, it seemed.

—Did you listen, Sire, to my tale?

—Every word.

—And, Sire?

—What happened the couple?

—*What happened the couple?*

30

Froth of mirth across unconscionable outrage.
—Yes.
—Quotidian bliss, Sire, decades—at the usual rates.
Wicked now. Consenting adults. And wicked.
—And what does it mean?
—*What does it mean?*
—Yes, the meaning —
—None, Sire.
—None—at all?
—Sire, if you insist —
—I do.
Pause.
—Behold a bubble, Sire, with claws—no harm to it unless
encountered by dusk.
—And if encountered by dusk?
—Better if should happen to one than two. And better to
two than three.
Mark's eyes drank of the forest.

—When Iseult and I sailed from Ireland we each had a
garment specially chosen and laid apart from the rest—two
shifts white as snow. That was a hot voyage. Iseult took to
wearing her shift all the time—in that heat she couldn't bear
anything else on her body. Naturally, it became soiled from
constant use—while mine, unused, remained spotless. We
arrived here, Iseult married the king, and was about to go to
bed with him. Her shift was not as she would have liked it to
be. I gave her mine. Unless she's now annoyed with me for
that, I don't know how else I may have upset her.
That was what Brangwen said when the two men drew
weapons to kill her.
—Tell her what I've said, and that I love her, she added.
The men relented. They tied Brangwen high in a tree (as
protection against wolves), cut out the tongue of one of their
dogs, and returned to Iseult.
—Her tongue, Madame.
Curl of pink on the broad palm: Iseult looked up from it.
—What did she say?
—That when you and she sailed from Ireland you each had

31

a garment apart—two spotlessly white shifts. The voyage was hot. You took to wearing your shift all the time, you couldn't—such was the heat—bear anything else on your body. You arrived here, married the king, and were about to go to bed with him. Your shift—from constant use on the voyage—was not as you would have liked it to be. Brangwen gave you hers, it had remained unused, it was spotlessly clean.

Iseult studied the blunt faces.

—And you've killed her?

—As you ordered, Madame.

—The two of you will hang.

—You ordered her killed, Madame.

—I sent her with you to fetch herbs for my headache.

—You ordered her killed, Madame.

—You'll both hang.

—She lives, Madame.

—She lives?

—Lives, Madame.

—Bring her to me.

The men looked at Iseult.

—Bring her here.

—Iseult, you strange person . . .

When Brangwen was brought back from the forest, Iseult kissed and embraced her over and over. That storm passed. Brangwen stepped back.

—Iseult, you strange person . . .

Iseult gave herself to the open window, the beech in the garden, the wind's touch light on it, resonant whisper of the foliage running from rim to rim and off into the air.

—Going, going, going, yet never moves at all, Tristan?

—The road.

—Climbs the rock, Tristan, no feet, no bones, no drop of blood?

—The mist.

—Clear sky, Tristan, never a cloud?

—Mirror.

—A man that's not a man kills a bird that's not a bird?

Stymied by Mark.

32

—Two ends in the water, Tristan, its middle dry?
—Bridge.
—Through the sea without drowning, through the fire with-
out burning?
—Sunlight.
—Greasy strap, Tristan, under the ground?
—Snake.
—Old as the mountains, Tristan?
—The valleys between.
—A man that's not a man kills a bird that's not a bird with
a stone that's not a stone?
Stymied.
—White white lady, Tristan, fire on her head?
—Candle.
—Breast but no nipple, Tristan?
—Egg.
—Cuts, cuts, sheds no blood, Tristan?
—Boat before the wind.
—Everyone doing it at the same time, Tristan?
—Growing old.
—A man that's not a man kills a bird that's not a bird with
a stone that's not a stone in a tree that's not a tree?
Stymied—but lashed back.
—Often seen where it isn't?
Mark stared.
—Often seen where it isn't?
Stared.
—*Blame, blame, blame.*

They remembered that long after but remembered more his
replies that first day when someone or other had not so
innocently asked —
—And what do you do in your spare time, Tristan?
—I ramble the woods.
—What do you do in the woods?
—I count the trees.
—How many trees in the wood, Tristan?
—Two.
—Name them.

33

—The green. And the withered.

In the seductive voice he kept polished for any or all occasions.

—Two, says he. The green. And the withered.

The Man-Keeper

They were cutting the hay this day. He was pleased—he was generally pleased—and a little drowsy from the heat. He lay down to rest on the fresh grass, leaving the men to it, and dozed off. When he awoke the day was far gone and there was no one in the field but himself.

He rose and made his way home to dinner feeling a little out of sorts: the sleep hadn't refreshed him at all. In the house he decided against having dinner.

—You don't feel well? the daughter asked.

—I don't feel right, he said, I feel like the bed, and that's where I'm going.

—You were working too hard, you tired yourself.

He explained that he'd had a long sleep in the field.

—You've a bit of a chill from lying on the fresh grass, you'll be fine in the morning.

He took the night's sleep but in the morning he felt worse, and complained of a kind of backward and forward movement in his stomach. When evening came and there wasn't the least sign of improvement, they sent for the doctor. The doctor came and questioned and examined. He listened at length to the troubled stomach.

—Now, the patient called out. Can't you hear the backwards and forwards of it?

The doctor could hear nothing.

—He's imagined the whole thing, he told the wife and daughter. He'll be all right in a few days, I believe, but let me know.

He left a bottle, and departed.

There was no improvement in a few days; the stirring inside had gone away—that was all that could be said. The doctor was sent for once more, and came several days running. In the end he confessed himself baffled, said he'd come no more, and refused to take a penny for his services.

The house was in a state. A second doctor was sent for, and a third, and a fourth. They came singly, and they came in a bunch. They flourished long names for the illness, prescribed potions and ointments, and charged a lump of money for their attentions, which were to no avail whatever. Quack-doctors followed the doctors, one came striding over every hill: they muttered and made signs and left powders and distillations and didn't forget to charge either. The patient continued to fade. Six months had passed: look at him now and all you saw was shadow in a bottle.

Summer came again. The invalid had a habit of sitting by the door a few hours a day in good weather. He was sitting there one day when along came a travelling-woman he knew. They greeted each other, and the travelling-woman couldn't but say what she felt.

—You're a changed man since I saw you last.

—I'm sick, he told her, I'm more than sick, and no cure in the world.

—Doctors?

—They've taken half the farm, and for what?

—Healers?

—Robbers all.

He told her the whole story, how he'd fallen asleep on the fresh grass that day, the upset that followed, all the comings and all the goings.

—Fresh grass?

—Fresh grass.

—Moist maybe?

—No, no.

—A stream close by?

—Yes, a stream close by.

—Can you show me the spot?

The spot. It was the last place he wanted to see. Even as she asked, he remembered that it must be up on a year to the day since he'd risen from sleep and walked away from it. His grave. Must he go with her to point out his grave? He dragged himself to the field. He showed her the exact spot; the hay had just been cut, and the fresh grass shone. The travelling-woman studied closely the various weeds and herbs growing there, and before

long stood up with a small juicy-looking herb between her
fingers.

—Do you see that?

—I do.

—Wherever you find that herb you won't have far to look
for what's bothering you.

—Go on.

—You've swallowed a man-keeper.

The travelling-woman met the wife and daughter and gave
them her information, and her advice.

—There's only one man can save him and that's The Prince
of Coolavin.

—And where's he to be found? the wife asked.

—On the brink of Lough Gara, it's three days from here, no
great journey.

A long discussion commenced. The wife and daughter were
in favour of making the journey; anything that offered hope
must be tried. The invalid was the obstacle: he'd had enough
of doctors—and others, he couldn't be cured, he was too weak
to travel, let him die in peace. The discussion started over.
Finally, the three women convinced him to try it.

The four of them set out the next day, travelling by horse-
and-cart, loaded with provisions. They found lodgings the first
night and the second night. They took their fill of rest, especially
the invalid, who required constant care. On the third day they
arrived at the house of The Prince of Coolavin, a fine house on
the brink of the lake. They found the owner at home and the
invalid told his story.

—Fresh grass you slept on?

—Fresh grass it was.

—A stream close by?

—A stream close by, yes.

—You've swallowed a man-keeper.

The Prince was having his dinner—the main course that day
was corned beef. He sat the invalid down at the table, put a
great helping of the corned beef before him, and commanded
him to eat. The invalid thanked him but drew back—he'd eaten
nothing in months, he couldn't touch it.

—Eat that if it was to choke you.

37

Forced to it, he got through a third of the plate.

—Fine, said The Prince, rest yourself for a few hours now.

In the late afternoon The Prince led him out to a field near the house. The three women followed. There was a stream running through the field. The Prince put him lying down on the bank of the stream, face directly above the water, mouth open and very close to the water.

—Whatever happens, said The Prince, don't move.

The invalid nodded.

The Prince withdrew, and joined the women a few yards back.

Nothing happened for quite a while. At the end of an hour the invalid felt something stirring inside him, first a backwards and a forwards, then making—at a guess—for the spoon of the breast, on in the direction of the throat, next in his mouth, moving out to the tip of the tongue, next no move at all. About a minute later he felt a stirring in his mouth again, the dart out to the tongue-tip, and this time *plop* with it into the water.

—Don't move, The Prince warned.

The invalid didn't move. In a few minutes he experienced a repeat of the stirrings, first the backwards and forwards, then making headway, up into the mouth, out to the tip of the tongue, sliding back, no move at all, forward again, and *plop* again into the water. It was a procession after that, a dozen in all.

—There's your clutch, said The Prince, now for the mother.

The invalid was close to exhaustion, and growing fretful. When another hour passed without incident, he made to rise, he could take no more. The Prince and the travelling-woman had to go forward and forcibly hold him down, one to each shoulder: there they stayed. The wife and daughter, pale the pair, watched from their same station.

A short time passed, and the invalid felt a stirring inside that surpassed anything so far, a stirring that was almost a tearing, forcing its way up to the throat, through and into the mouth, and resting there. The invalid moved. His hand shot to his mouth but, if he was quick, the man-keeper was quicker: back down the throat with her, gone.

—Didn't I tell you not to move? snapped The Prince, you've

maybe frightened her for good.

But he hadn't. She came up again in about twenty minutes, the same tearing and pushing, up into the mouth, timidly there for a minute or two, scouting, back and forth, back and forth, out at last to the tip of the tongue, and *plop*—seven times the plop of any of the others—into the water.

—Well you knew the tub of butter when you found it, The Prince roared after her.

They carried the invalid back to the house. He said nothing for three hours. The first words he said were:

—I'm a new man.

The Harper's Turn

The most beautiful one ever wind or sun played on.

Dance for your Daddy
my little babby
dance for your Daddy
my little lamb

you'll have a fishy
in your little dishy
you'll have a fishy
when his boat comes in

you'll have a brush
and you'll have a comb
you'll have a rattle—

And when she found his body she sucked the wounds, drank, there, took to the wilds, grew hair, fur, killer-claws, struck as she pleased man and beast, sucked ever and always, sucked the wounds, drank them dry.

Spills of light teemed in the crevices of a stone wall. The old man drifted along the face of it. His hand rose, slipped between blue stones, searched, withdrew, over and over. There wasn't a sound. The wall swallowed the drifting hand, held, released it. The spills of light warmed the hand, touched the old man as he moved along.

Not his room but it owned him. He was hooped above a bubbling pot. A cat was being boiled. The door was pushed open. A wolf entered, looked at him clearly.

—That's witch's work.

She presented a strangled stag.

He cut the stag's throat, skinned it, quartered it.

He made a fire, put granite stones in it.

He dug a hole, filled it with water.

He wrapped the meat, put it in the hole, fed the stones, cooked the meat.

They ate.

He stood her in the hole where the lukewarm broth and the melted fat of the stag was and massaged her every part and worked the broth and the oils and the juices over her and into her until sweat broke and poured.

He made a bed for her, he spread the hide of the stag under her and his cloak above her.

—I prefer to have her brought in alive—that's just me.

—Your love sounds are tropical birds.

—Take my eyes.

—Rewards galore. Victims also.

—And hands.

—Asleep you know all the lines leave your face.

—The world's full of bad harpers.

—Last night I heard a lovely story—from myself.

A white stag crossed his path more than once.

—Who are you?

Woman he would have halted: on her forehead a profusion of curls but glossy bald the back of her head. What she said was no help.

—Make a fist in your pocket. Continue the ritual.

She presented
he cut
he made
he wrapped
fed the stones
he stood
he took
he rubbed
he made
he spread.

41

Fur fell away, claws, all fell away, again before him and all sun and wind the most beautiful.

His chin with a trick of swerving betimes slightly as rue on the smile to ride some anticipated blow.

—What is it you look for?

—Words that will stick in my throat.

She saw him day after day pulling a shadow inside him. Sometimes she wanted to wash his feet. That had happened before.

Often and often I had a wish to wash his feet, bathe them, wash them, dry them, he wanted me to, I knew that unspoken, I never did, there's one of my should haves, windfall now under the tree.

—What are you thinking?

—The way that river digs. The gape of the ford.

He played for her.

She took his hands, kissed his eyes.

—Once I was with a girl and we saw—imagine the ugliest savage of a dog you can imagine. What breed was it? She went up to ask. Leaning, she patted the dog. At once the dog was gentle, a wonderful shape. The two made a picture. I shrank before it.

—I love you like a spectator, my love.

Gravely she walked beside him. They were expected—a large crowd had gathered, swelled at their approach. There was no surprise—everything was known, it appeared, everything arranged.

They murdered him.

The king stared away.

She looked at the ground.

—Speak to us, won't you?

Her brown foot played the grass. She watched it part the lush stems, bare fraught roots. She stood there. She listened. Her whole head listened and heard.

42

Sweeney Among The Branches

The glen had doors to the four quarters but there you were among your own, feathered all, designing in the air paths (or cancelling paths), sliding from tree to curl of rock, alighting to quarrel or caress or riffling in flight the water of clear pools, and ballyrag ceaseless, clawing for the pick of the water cress, the smoothest banks, suntraps, leeward cnoceens, every tree here and populous every tree.

A group of women, how beautiful their hair, a man among them playing with the hair of each in turn, that dark hair he takes, binds his wrists, slowly frees, lets it away, this brown-red he gathers high, lets fall, gathers again, lets fall, with the hair of this other he covers his face, the fine fair hair masking, softening to silk, the jut of the face.

Oak: two acorns floating, stirred by the wind . . .
Elder: necklace of nine berries a cure.
Pine: crane roosting within.
Beech: thin boards for the secret song.
Aspen: why should we tremble?
Ash, elm, sycamore, birch, hazel, fir, blackthorn, yewy yew.

The miller came on tracks he recognised on the bank of a stream where water cress grew and was being plucked, and came also on branches fresh-broken—that was the charging from the top of one tree to another but no sign of the party.

Exhausted, the miller went into a deserted house, lay down and slept. Thus there were tracks to the house. Thus the miller was watched while he slept.

Odours of the mill. And the miller's wife's giving hand. The miller glimpsed a shadow by the mill-stream.

—A visitor?

—Here last night.

43

The miller wearing his wife's mother's clothing settled in the mill for the night, knitting, pretending to knit, arranging, re-arranging his wife's mother's cloak about his shoulders, smoothing the skirt, minding the tongs from the fire.

Sighting and visiting and searching clefts and cavities, spinning from estuary to estuary, peak to peak, glen to glen, gulp now the bellowing of the stags, foxes' barking, badger's squeal, a morning heron's lifted wings, apples, berries, nuts, herbs for the taking, early days early days, grey branches stretch, cold for roof, cold for bed, frost ahead which will name every pool, and Merlin's laughter spilling from the woods—*All corn wheat, all metal gold, all birth yours*—that was the trouble with Merlin's laughter.

—We spoke mostly of you.
(Thanks.)
—*What about the marvels?*
—We are ashamed —
—Ashamed —
—That you should be seen —
—As you are —
—By those who knew you —
—As you were.
Shout above the shouts: *Your home is in the east—not the west.*
—*The marvels?*
Mean them.

The top of a tall ivied hawthorn. Every twist a dose of the harrow. Roost elsewhere. In sight under an old moon thicket of briars swollen with waiting, single blackthorn in the middle rising clear and clarion. To the tip of the blackthorn in the middle of the swollen with waiting. The blackthorn holds, sways, holds. The blackthorn gives. All thorns needle and tear. Floor of the thicket. Skin pumping. Warm ooze of the blood.

The miller my brother: thick sleep of the snore, the face of all idle and known as the cap and the spade, known weather, known road, known plot of ground—lure of it, numb of it, stoop of it, lure of its rise and torpid lie down.

By this well. One strolled from the house nearest. Skip to a yew. Calmly she plucked watercress, cleared the lot.
—Why not the water while you're at it?
The smile: eel-grass after a spring-tide storm.
—I have water, watercress, and trees.
—Call my handful a gift to The Lord.
—Split it with the miller when you two meet.

Sir:
When I was a child I was sent to your people. A woman of my people was sent with me. You banished her. A woman of your people took over. This was the woman who left me alone in the garden. The bees rose up. I was stung in the eye. Once I killed an enemy of yours. Dying, he flung the chess-piece he held so that he broke the crooked eye in my head. You ask what I want? I want your blue eye and your fair right hand.

Late afternoon shadow of a hare melting in a gap of November.

Circling a house. Staring the windows. Finding the door. Knocking. Listening. Entering. Establishing the house empty. Finding a room. Entering a room. Viewing a bed, undressed, robe, hair-brush, scattered shoes. Drinking that room. Leaving that room, house, weak in the body.

—Who are you?
—Another one.
—Shake.
—Do I know you?
—Look at me.
—The black lake has disturbed you.
—Knife that on the stone.
—There was a battle imminent. I argued that none should go unless beautifully dressed—silk shirts and cravats, verdant tweed jackets, peacock boots, hose that shone.

45

—They turned on you?
—Drove me to where you found me.
—How will you die?
—A blast of wind, a waterfall. And you?
—A morning seduction.

Fir: boughs thrashing each other, the air, all comers, and eat before dawn the seeds of that cone.

The frost-bird flew, white iron the cut of the world, earth rang, water stared, breath swivelled, they gaped from the trees: *Who owned it?* named frost-fern and frost-itch, frost-dew and frost-bow and frost-smoke a weight on the sea, named them as strangers: it gathered: black frost and white, diamond and button and wreathing a chain, they ate of the rime but not tasting, stung cheek-bones they humped there, morning struck morning and etched in the trees they cursed blood, they dwindled, white hurricane stirred, white hurricane lifted, white hurricane blew, they bowed, well, some bowed, and that morning, coldest of all, roused to the known: frost-bird was flying, white scorched the white, marrow flamed, they tasted, they knew it for theirs—their fire, their anvil, their shape that would be, their smoke from the rib, their fern in the glass.

—Send for the miller.
Word spread, a mob flowered.
—Send for the miller.
The miller came, stood under the tree, took aim, conferred, took aim.
—I have news for you.
No reply.
—Your mother's dead.
No reply.
—Did you hear me?
Nothing. Murmur through the crowd. The miller looked at them, stillness, he spoke again to the branches.
—Would you hear of your sister?
No reply.
—Your sister, I said?

46

—I know of my sister.
—She's won't speak your name.
—I know of my sister.
—What do you know?
—The mild sun rests on every ditch —
The crowd swayed, driving the miller against the tree, shouts
from the crush, an altercation stifled, the silence leaned again
to the voice from the branches.
—A sister loves though she be not loved.
They juggled that. The miller steadied.
—Have you heard of your daughter?
Nothing.
—She lies by your mother.
Nothing.
—Did you hear what I said?
He fell from the tree.

Islands: a memory, islands like cats on the warm morning
rug of the sea.
Somewhere a glass of wine, red wine, flung, running warm
on the face, her lips then, tongue, licking and kissing it away.
To foot it in hailstones, mind always on early departure.

—Up there space only.
—Can you leap now?
—Don't tempt me.
—Can you though?
—Don't.
—Can you?
Across the bed-rail.
—Leap that myself.
Through the skylight.
—Leap that too.
Play resumes. The air flume and you're one with the flood
again.
It was harvest. Succulent evening light. The land tilted and
swayed. Houses firm at their moorings. The hag stuck in.
Plain, bog, mountain, up and across, the flow cataract, breath
seized, until the sea called dark in and hip to hip they made for

47

the headland as though for home, it watched them come, knew them well, and they swung to the peak, still two in the race, and flake down the black breast of the cliff and out into the tide and fading, all right, yield to the swell, yield, but one only in the race now, a pack of her *Regard stay clear regard* a pack of her own gather the bits from the strand, burn those you'll have wise ashes.

Tall figure standing sharp as a blade on the ditch but pale underworked face. Scatter of men and women unkempt on the road. Mute event. Lips of the one in charge mobile and gestures but nothing to be heard; those on the road nodding, jostling, thinning piecemeal. A pair gone in anger, another off to a torn smile, another aside to stare the shabby sea. Scuds of rain, the light a brown streak on the heads of the bidders. Now four left, three, two, males back to back, nodding, no give, the one in charge patters on, no give, a cool bitter contest glimpsed in passing. Earth for sale? Air? Water? Watercress? The water's green blossom, given of quiet that grows as it yields.

Ash: your shadow my pulse of waiting.
Hazel: come by night.
Birch: those seven sons with hats of birch returning.
Alder: don't fell it.
Yew: coffin of the vine.

—Do you remember?
—I want to be with you.
—You seek me?
—I live in this doorway.
—Enjoy him?
—I want you.
—White stone for pillow?
—Come in and eat.
—How did you know me?
—The step of you.
—He's the chosen one now.

—Come let me feed you.

Last glimpse of her leaning against a doorpost watching the arrival of number one, rubbing her foot against a doorpost.

Cold wind springing from the peaks of each mountain, chilly the dart of morning *Your body will be a feast for birds of prey / Ravens your heavy silence,* bent the nails, worn the loins, pierced the feet, raw the thighs, the house gapes, this is the seat, a comfortless unquiet place, heart of storm the only shelter.

It would be Friday. Line of women in a field by the river beating flax. Hooped backs, bare arms rise and fall, supple flow to the work: a beat commencing, travelling the line, starting over, no looking up: *Spin, damn ye, spin, spin.* Off to one side a woman lying alone opened her legs, sped into labour.

—Where are you coming from?
—Where I left.
—Where are you bound for?
—Where I'm going.

Five trunks hopping all over the road, headless, the severings red circles that shone in the murk, and the five heads of the trunks skipping a pattern beside them, glinting faces, and five more, five grizzle-heads without body or trunk screaming and leaping the road. The fifteen drove on, five trunks and five heads and five without body or trunk. They followed, braying —

—Smell your bones.
—We'll parcel you in timber.
—When you're dead there's no world.

And now the five trunks and the five heads and five without body or trunk were goat-head and dog-head and wolf-head, chopping at calves, houghs, thighs, shoulders, nape of neck. Head clashed with head, with trees, spikes of rock. Out for a kill, they rose lumps but he shed the pack, lost them, left them lost as himself in steeps of the sky.

Spray clearing the cliff-top, curtains that tangled and fell and were flung high again. He watched: he saw the change, along the cliff-top in regular formation three, six, a dozen spouts of

49

water clear against the sky, spout after spout, twice a man's
height, say, the crests foaming. He watched: he saw these seed
the channel below, whitecaps shaped there became jet in turn,
plumed and holding, and now at a free ordered pace the whole
channel was yielding, the water a weave of fountains extending
as it came. This design asked for nothing, it played, and all his
joints made welcome. The advancing line was quite close now.
One jet lifted above the others, was column, a tower, the crown
foam. The water-pillar watched him. He watched: he saw drops
from the height, droplets, coast free, carry towards him, one,
a single one touched his forehead, the sea calmed.

There's a corpse hanging from the tree.
I cut the rope.
It thumps to the ground.
It moans.
I turn it over.
It bursts out laughing.
—Why do you laugh?
It's back on the branch.
I take breath.
I cut the rope again.
It thumps to the ground.
It lies there.
It moans.
I say nothing.
I shoulder the load.
It speaks again.
—Friend, you like riddles?
I say nothing.
—Are you one for the riddles?
I say nothing.
—Here's a riddle to shorten your journey—if you know the
answer and don't speak your head will explode, all right?

—Give him some of each day's milking.
One of the milk-yard women was put in charge of the
arrangement. Soon there was talk. The husband speared him
in the left nipple as he was stretched out sipping the milk.

50

Muirghil was the woman's name. It was her habit to thrust her heel up to the ankle in the cowdung—a quiet part of the yard—and leave the fill of that of fresh milk for him morning and evening.

Cliodhna's Wave

One towards whom the men came with stones in their sleeves.
One who made, as directed, for the shore, and saw the currach
appear, high in the bow and with a stern of copper, two young
men abroad, each one robed shoulder to heel.
—Will you take me?
—If you're quite alone.
One who stepped into the sea and sprang abroad and was
taken away.
One for grief of whom women pegged hatchets at the sea.

A haystack bursting into flame: no one next or near. Cows
licking the seaweed. And The Fish whispering: *The fish rots
head first.*

—You're a duck, she said. You can go under for as long as
you like. That's one of your eyes.
—And the other?
—A keyhole.
She spoke distractedly all evening. Then, towards midnight,
—My hands are ruined.

To see your face in the rapids, that's, they say, the surest
sign.

The green severities of the sea. Matters at the worst, a rider
on a pale-grey horse rose out of the heave and whip, horse and
rider dry as the floor of the oven. They must bow. They bowed.
He lifted them on to the horse, nudged the reins.
—It's always desirable to have two notions, the voice so level
commended, one to demolish the other.
The currach turned on its side, followed them across the
waves.

—What about that bird?

On a high sill a bird with beak of iron and tail of fire. It rattled plumage. Everywhere weapons fell. Those who picked them up stiffened on the spot, stuck there. The rod of copper—taken from the currach—was handy. It cut the air. The bird fell.

—What remains then but to go to her?

—Who are you?

—Just one thing: speak to her from the ends of your bones.

The tall one moved off, water slopping from the thigh-high boots.

—I'm Sweet-One-Day and Sour-The-Next.

A cat that coughed and spewed a fog of ashes through the place.

The fiddler, plying his bow across a shank of bone that shone white and cast a red shadow.

—I'm three by three, the fiddler cried, Crooked against Crooked, Corner against Corner, and Trick against Treachery.

And:

—If I promised to bring it *to* you, I did not promise to bring it *for* you.

So they met.

Her smooth side to him.

His smooth side to her.

—Mine at the ebb and mine at flood tide.

—Mine at the ebb and mine at flood tide.

Before they left there was that gift of a cup, green and shapely.

—This will tell you what to drink.

Cliodhna observed the play.

—Where was it made?

—A whale that was washed ashore here. When we cut him up we found that in the heart. Se we call it *The Product of The Beast*.

That straightened your eyes all right.

The morning shone on them.

—You've dolphin hands.

—Listen: I can tell it only to the trees . . .

—But I hear . . .

Their kisses turned to birds.

The Boyne beckoned: they were bound for The Palace of The God of Love. From the heaps of the deep the eels whistled fair wind and good tide. Ireland came into view. The land breeze. Smoke, blossom, clay. The Boyne. Waterford, Wexford, hills playing with the sea. The leak in his heart gaped. He lulled her to sleep. He turned the currach. Sole of the oar and palm of the oar. She slept like a thrush. He rounded Ireland south-about and kept going until he came to the harbour of Glandore. He'd land here and find food. He moored the currach, looked at her sleeping, kissed bright hair that stirred to the breeze.

—You've taken away the look of my life.

Whisper, and he slipped ashore. As he stepped into the forest he heard the howl of the wave. A branch cut him across the eyes.

—Lick lips for your supper.

Also one who loved animals. When he died his cattle gathered about the body. They nosed, they tugged, they poked. With their horns they tore him to pieces, stampeded a province, and, reaching The Boyne, paused there to slake thirst, to taste of Boann The Beautiful, that Boann who dared the burdened pool, drew from it three volumes of water—at the cost of an eye, an arm, and a thigh, turned seaward to hide her disgrace, and—the waters eager and at one—seaward was borne.

The Hospital Barber

The magic cow—sieve there instead of bucket—gave until she bled, cut loose, tore a gap in the rim of the valley, and vanished into the sea near Howth.

—Get it out of there—if only for cosmetic reasons.
(Cosmetic, mind you.)
—It's your cyst, all the same to me.
—Damage likely?
—No.
—What's your advice?
—Your cyst.
The hospital barber: *Christ, you're a hairy man.*
—Why?
—Just pop up. Live a thousand years you mightn't get another on that spot.
—Take it out.
Done. And, lo and behold, another pops up on the same one, two new ones for more than good measure on the left, epidydimal harvest, *sub rosa*.
—Feel lighter now?
—Oh considerably.

Heavy traffic, thunder and lightning, holding that child in his arms, sheltering, a good feeling and a bad, mind the child, mind the child, ever walk across a cobbled yard a wine-glass tied to your ankle, the child a fragile old dog for the hard road had been pulled out of ditches, quagmires, marl-holes and midden-humps, indestructible, breath, clay, open hand, and telegram-boy—*Frog needs no hammer in the rainy season* . . .

A land dispute, yet another, warning letters by the dozen, and the father had a dream, no, met a ghost while walking the road: the dog refused to pass the gate of the broad field, stood

55

there trembling, and the father knew, leaned over the gate, looked right under the hedge, an old man sitting there, stranger, wearing plain as plain—the father recognised it at once—the hat of the grandfather long dead and gone—*Mind your own business*. On the Monday morning, as previously announced, Mark entered the field, commenced to plough, and the sniper, all for symmetry, allowed him three furrows, then—British Army trained—shot the horses, first the white, next the grey, next Mark through the forehead, they heard the shots, the father found him, neighbours refused water, their need greater than his.

—You sound tense?

She admires herself before the mirror like Diane de Poitiers— some Actaeon gallivanting to his noon appointment, skin 'em and ate 'em, a wise animal, a shore creature, but why keep knocking glasses, breaking mirrors?

—You steal all my best stories.

In that land the old were young the young old, the old one banged whatever was handy with whatever was handy and shouted—When I was young, when I was young . . . I was in my alley then . . .

Dawn-light or thereabouts (this child takes minding) and a garden, sliding away from the garden a woman and her daughter, the garden pool, a dog surfacing, friend, pointer, swims clear, white and brown, and is the child who strolls where wild orchids, winnowed blue, lacemaker texture, grow: among them, turn of the hand, breath, he gathers pollen, pollen, pollen, ambles on.

Sionnan

Sionnan lived in The Land Under Wave not far from Connla's well where the fish was. Nine streams flowed from that well, nine hazels around it, and the hazels let fall leaf, blossom, and fruit in the one stroke, and the fish ate of the fruit. You mustn't touch the fish. She went to the well at noon, the fish basking there. She reached, she touched, and the well rose, and the nine streams rose, and the waters pitched her into the upper world. That was the end of Sionnan, start of the river that carries her name.

Parading the street him and her, two of them in it, wearing (fresh from the accident) matching neck-braces to impressive effect. While in the house the one new-born is weighed hourly: lifted from the cot, placed on the scales, a reading noted, returned to the cot.

Every time the mouth opens this rivulet of double negatives.

—I wouldn't say I wouldn't.

—I couldn't say I couldn't.

—I shouldn't say I shouldn't.

And that woman, when she spoke her long left arm swung, flapped counter-point to the beat of her words, long red-sleeved arm, the left, something else again.

—Any good news?

—A stridable day. The word *watersmeet*.

—Yes?

—The runic in her gaze.

—All to the living-room.

The youngsters assemble.

Another grave question-and-answer (and listen) session, he will question, they speak plain, sibling fret, Dad's bulk, life at the door.

—Put on your masks.

One by one they put on their masks, home-made, various, a stocking, a paper bag, a torn straw-hat (once the mother's), a hallow-e'en relic of a mask.

—Now, with whom shall we begin?

—Just as I stepped into the house with the head of cabbage a big lump of a frog ripe yellow slips from it, floats to the parquet, looks about, and—two hops—lands behind the door.

—Throw it on the fire?

—I went white. But I reached behind the door, lifted it up— this balloon, soft and cold—and took it outside and left it in the long grass.

—Lick it?

—No.

—Should have.

—Should?

—I've just dreamed the most beautiful dream I've ever dreamed.

Transformed, she was speaking to her father transformed. They were in a royal forest, standing beside his coffin. He was dead and coffined but also standing there transformed. There was a box on the lid of the coffin, a chest, in it a child's night-things, a pillow, a rug. A child came to sleep there every night.

—One who is not aflame cannot burn, her father said.

And look at the end of Mick Maille that was once a dandy, martyr for the women, had his education, bit of a poet in his own way. Found him stiff on the floor that was covered in pitch he had in cans there for treatin' round-sticks, it was all over him, that took scrubbin', round-sticks, I ask you, that he could plunge in the land to fence the beasts, and this pitch— I'll smell it forever in that kitchen—to treat the timber, keep it from rot, the god-damn round-sticks rotten to start with, but anything he found on the shore he brought home under the oxter, never fret, a comical class of a gent that took hard scrubbin' at the latter end.

Sionnan, my love, spread your wings, spread your wings.

Occasion of Note

There she lay.

—The last time I saw you I remember it as well as well, scatter-brain priest in the back of the church, and jigged as he sang, The last time I saw you you were carrying an ingrown toe-nail, this ingrown toe-nail, you were hopping with the dart of it, lepping out of your skin, amn't I right now, amn't I? I remember it as well as well.

—Ingrown toe-nail?

—Amn't I right now, amn't I?

Well, maybe the man was right.

Quotations innumerable . . . *She should have died hereafter | There would have been a time for such a word . . . Vanessa scarce in years a score | Dotes on a gown of forty-four . . .* Then fewer.

—Try the walls.

Old man hunkered in the grey of a corner.

—Try them, touch them.

The spot spilled to a touch—powder, shook his head but his heart shook before.

The living-room rectangular, low-ceilinged, not an encouragement, at the far end a group of women, lean arrangement of forms which swung towards him, one—recognition crisp about her—advanced, and he left, tossing a sour *mea culpa,* not daring to look back.

—Try them, touch them.

It showered rain. He looked up. The ceiling was stuccodore magic, beauty of line deferring to a central circle. The rain fell, and he stood there letting it take him face up, eyes on the ceiling all the time.

That girl in the red dress, girl of the village when he was

doing his spell in the far north, one evening by the window spoke back to him as the light fell away, *The time will come, listen to me now, the time will come when you'll remember this time as the happiest time of your life.*

Out of the tepid hysteria of the crowd came a man, stared into his eyes, rummaged there.
—She often spoke of you.
—I suppose.

The door was shut but it was given him to see through and— tasting the flavour of his advantage—he could watch her moving about, sniffing her next step, this door, that, which, and the air of business to be completed. He looked quickly towards the corner. The old man still there. Her clipped steps on the hall flag-stones. Mouth tight, he waved to the old man, *Help me, help me.* The old man didn't move, calmly regarded him, made no move at all.

Perhaps you don't hate yourself enough?

Everything adhered. You walked downstairs and through a tunnel to board for the journey back, night train to the west, only a few drunks and the mail, under your arm a trout, deep-freeze trout, gift from the brother and the lakes of the central plain, deep-freeze under your oxter on your way to the sea where mackerel skies and mares' tails make tall ships shorten sails.

Left Of The Door

Take the can, a stiff arm, take the can, fixing eyes high on walls, on doors. Creak of the can, your steps, rattle-and-click of the outer door. Step outside, sour May cold, slap of the wind, and stand stiff as a board. The spade left of the door. Eyes fixed, keeping the eyes at eye-level, reach, and gather the spade with the left hand, and turn, and past the kitchen window, dragging open the small gate, crossing the lane, and stepping on to the dung-heap. And advancing to the middle of the dung-heap, stand.

Looking away, leave down the can on a level spot. Do it quick. Grip the spade, and scrabble on the face of the dung-heap, root and scoop and hoke a spot, claw and tear. Drop the spade. Looking away, turn to the can. And take the can, and looking away, not looking away, spill it there, scorch of poor pink flesh-fish in the shit and the mess. Down the can, and grab the spade, and over it, cover it, maul and root dung back there, cover it, put more, that'll do, more, that'll do, leave it.

Take the can, spade and the can, turn away, stand up, lift your head, and fix on the sea, the stretch of it, the sea this day, rag where your chest was, and slap of the wind.

Step up on the dung-heap, and move to the middle. And stand and listen to yourself. Leave down the can on a level spot. Sprout looking up at you. Take the spade, and go to it, shoulder to the wind. Scoop, don't rush this, clear a basin in the dung-heap, give it shape, take time, you have time, your back a hard curve, face blind as the spade. Take your time. Leave down the spade. Turn to the can. Take the can, and care over what you're about, and watching, spill all into the basin, and look, and meet the whole slither and slop, blood and the mess and morsel raw on the dung. Turn away, and take the spade, and fill the basin, root on the cover of dung, and root

61

more, and secure it, and then some more, and leave it now. Lean on the spade, and fix on the stretch of sea.

Take the spade, and to it as they taught you, wield the spade, find a spot on the heap that will take the cut of the spade, moisture patch, and give it a rhythm, and make the small grave, know what you're about, good foot down and a foot by a foot, up on that, tidy it there, that'll do. Leave aside the spade. Go to the can. Stoop over it, and put in your hands. And lift out the sliver, slippery, and no weight, no weight at all, filmy man-woman of ours. Take it, dripping, and place in the one foot by one, set it there, scrap of her, lost bit. Go back to the can, and take the can, and again to the spot, and spill it all in. The dung drinks. The can aside. Pick up the spade. Sticky grip. 'Bye. And fill with care, using the spade as they taught you, finding the beat of it, letting the cut of the wind take your bones. Fill it, and fill it, and tend it, and more, and leave the spade aside. And down, and by the small heap, and feel it, and cry what you have for the was and the wasn't.

The can and the spade. Walk straight, child. Spade to the left of the door. Inside, the quiet, love, and the fire low.

Lovers Of The Island

We were the luck
We were the stepping-stones
We were the winners

Mushrooms in droves. Wild orchids proud in the long grass.
And the three fastest fish a bell in the tide.

He was out fishing with the men, the calmest day. The sea
turned rough. A big wave swept down on the boat. He took off
his shoe, flung it at the wave, and the wave fell away. Minutes
later the bigger wave. He took off the other shoe, flung it, and
the wave fell away. In no time the biggest wave. He grabbed
the bait-knife, flung it at the wave, and the whole sea calmed.
That evening he was alone in the cottage when there came a
knock on the door. He opened it to a stranger. The stranger
spoke —
—Will you come with me and take from my sister's heart the
knife you flung there today?
He hesitated.
—All right, he yielded, but no harm to me nor any of mine.
—Agreed.
They spun through the air, it could only have been seconds.
They landed before a door in the side of a mountain. They
entered and before them was a fine castle set among trees. The
stranger led him inside the castle and upstairs to a bedroom
where a beautiful young woman was lying with the bait-knife
stuck in her heart. She called to him —
—Will you come and take this knife from my heart that you
flung there today?
Again he hesitated.
—All right, but no harm to me nor any of mine.
—Agreed.
He drew out the knife, and she was healed.

63

He spoke to her —

—Why did you try to drown us today?

—I love you and want you.

She looked him full in the eye.

—And you'd drown the whole boat-load to have me?

—I love you and want you.

He studied her in awe. He'd never seen anyone more beautiful, never felt such power reaching. Again, he hesitated. Aching, he heard words that were his —

—That can't be.

In seconds he was back in the kitchen.

It seemed they were both of the island people. He was off on the mainland for the day. An old neighbour-woman came into the kitchen and stared at the floor.

—You have the skull of a horse down there.

—A sign of?

—Spring in the floor, good-luck at the door.

Later, walking the high road, she met The Skipper. He paused only to say —

—Long ago you had iron men on wooden ships. Nowadays you have wooden men on iron ships.

Next it was night but clear moonlight, and she was on the rocky shore of Bunamullen, the nearest bay on the northern side. A powerfully built young man stood between her and the water. His black hair shone. She watched him stoop, tie a rope about a large stone, and secure the other end about his neck and shoulders. He straightened and, bearing his stone, walked into the sea.

—How long for the body to rise? she was speaking to the old one who'd come by the cottage earlier.

—Nine days. It takes nine days for the brain to rot. The body's not heavy—it's the brain holds it down. If it wasn't for the brain, sky road was the road at your door.

Nor would they ever have known the island had not a father and son from the mainland been fishing one day in the long ago and discovered a great bank of fog some miles out. It was decided to rest and cook a meal. There was a bucket with embers. They fed the embers and cooked and ate some fish. The father flung the leavings of the fire into the sea. The fog lifted. There was an island. They went ashore. They came on a lake. By the lake were two beautiful fair-haired women, evidently mother and daughter. As the men approached, mother and daughter turned to a white cow and her calf—white-and-brown. The father told the son to get the calf. The son grabbed the calf's tail but tail and calf turned to a dribble of seaweed. When the father caught up with the white cow, she tipped him with a hind-hoof. He became a rock by the lake. And the cow vanished into the lake. Thus the island got its name. One of the oldest books makes mention of it: *There are two islands to the west of The Island of Britain, The Island of Ireland and The Island of Inishbofin, that is to say, The Island of The White Cow.*